ICEHOTEL™

Title ICEHOTEL™

Publisher JukkasAkademin AB
Author Pär Granlund
Cover Design Johan Lionell, Kraftverket Stockholm
Art Director Johan Lionell, Kraftverket Stockholm

Cover Photographer Peter Grant
Photographers Tomas Utsi, Peter Grant, Torbjörn Lövgren,
Eivon Carlsson, Per Svensson, Arne Bergh, Kai Piippo,
Christophe Lapetit, Per Nilsson

Creative Director Jan Rutenskiöld, Kraftverket Stockholm
Typographer Johan Lionell, Kraftverket Stockholm
Translation Mark Wilcox
Revision of text Novoterm Translation AB

Project manager Kerstin Andersson
Project assistant Karin Åberg

Paper MultiArt Silk 150 g/m^2 produced at Nymölla Mill,
Stora Enso Fine Paper
Printed in Milan by EUROLITHO Ltd
Repro Italgraf, Västerås

First Edition March 2000

JukkasAkademin AB
Köpmangatan 23B
SE-972 33 Luleå
SWEDEN
Phone +46 920 250 888
Fax +46 920 250 889

ISBN 91 630 8067 2

MultiArt – The natural Choice

MultiArt is a paper that reproduces text and picture in a natural way
with splendid lustre and depth. The result is first class, just like the
book you are holding in your hands right now. While you enjoy the
beautiful pictures from Icehotel in Jukkasjärvi think of MultiArt. It is
an important part of this exciting and exotic production.

MultiArt is produced by Stora Enso in substances from 90 to
300 g/m^2 in Silk and Gloss. It is a multi coated woodfree paper well suited
for books and printed matters that put high demands on picture and
colour reproduction.
MultiArt does not set the limits. The imagination does.

We wish you pleasant reading!   **Multi**Art

ICEHOTEL™

Late winter, one of the Eight Seasons of Lapland. The coming of the Midnight Sun is heralded by successively longer, brighter days.

Photo: Tomas Utsi

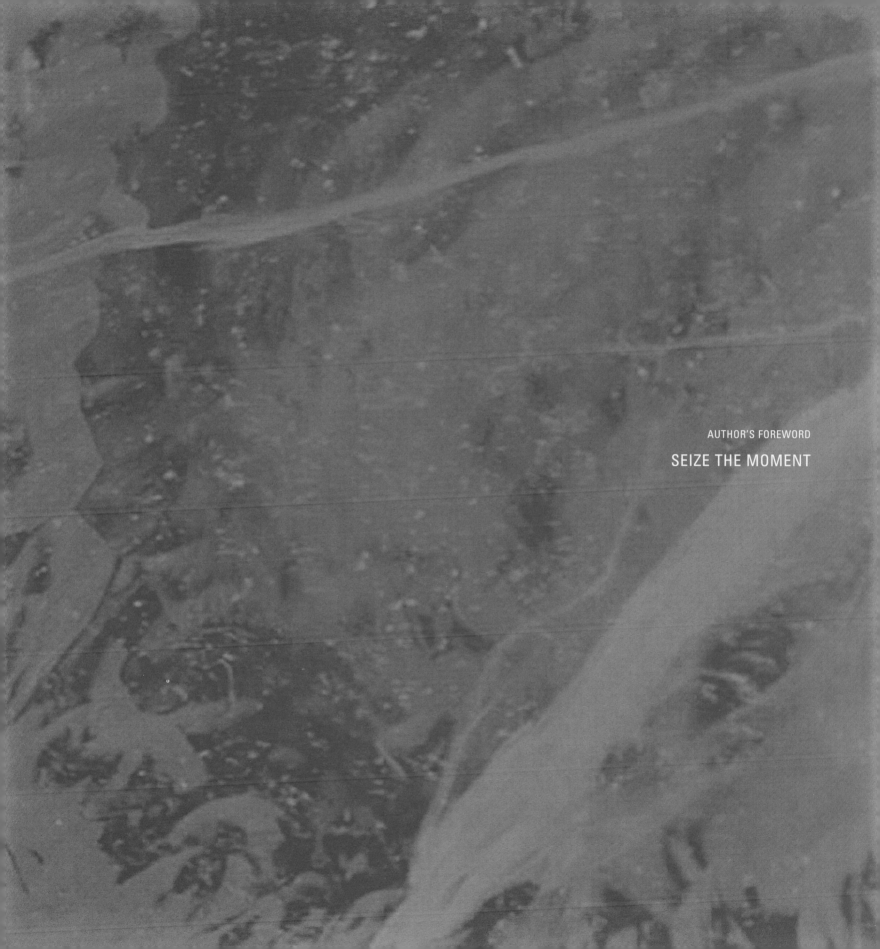

I don't know whether it is because life is too short or death is too long. The answer makes no sense, really. Like "Icehotel" and all the fabulous works of ice art that slowly melt back into pure water and flow back into the Torne River with the return of the Midnight Sun, my life, yours and everybody else's must one day come to an end.

That's why we must live for today and ad have the courage to seize the moment. Don't wait until tomorrow! Find the courage to go from thought to action! Live your life to the full and make your dreams come true! I hope you find the inspiration one cold winter's day during a visit to Icehotel, or from looking at the pictures in this book of the igloo in Jukkasjärvi.

Discover the magic and wonder of what might, at first, appear trifling and insignificant in the vast world around it, and experience the joy of seeing the huge and the magnificent inside something that it barely visible.

SEIZE THE MOMENT

In the face of biting cold and relentless wind, working day and night, ice builders and artists have created something big and magnificent – Icehotel – the structure itself, its interior and all its works of ice art. An infinite number of minuscule ice crystals, each one unique and beautiful, together form the snow and clear ice which constitute the roof and walls of the igloo.

In a way, every individual is a tiny ice crystal in the great ice hotel we call life. We are all just visiting. Just passing by – in the igloo and in life. Providence, chance, destiny – call it what you will – it can change our lives. For better or worse, I am convinced that we can make some sort of system out of chance; a positive and creative system. Encounters between people of different cultures, from different countries and varying walks of life, with common and uncommon interests, is one way of realizing this system. And this is exactly what happens again and again in the countless meetings between guests from all over the world at Icehotel. No one, apart from those involved, perhaps, can know the results of these unexpected meetings. They can, and often do, lead to long-term friendships and a better understanding of the lives of people from other backgrounds.

Even so, the exciting thing about life is that you don't always know what you don't know. If this wasn't the case, there would be no surprises or no new discoveries. And things generally stay this way until you meet a person who can tell you something interesting, new and unexpected. It is through the meetings of people in a positive, stimulating environment that new, sound ideas for developing our society are born. This world needs more such encounters.

Each year thousands of guests from all around the world meet at Icehotel. One of many common denominators is an attraction to this unique edifice of ice and snow. Those who come are open for new experiences. They are ready to be surprised by something they never knew existed until they heard rumours of the extraordinary structure in northern Sweden.

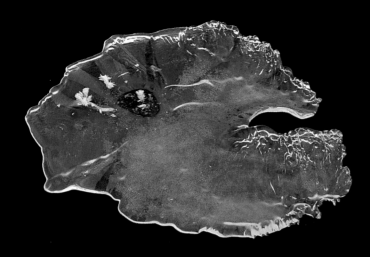

What's this? The art of discovering the beauty of the minuscule in the magnificent – and vice versa – created from pure water by the greatest of all ice sculptors — Nature.

Photo: Tomas Utsi

My chance meetings with Japanese visitors, with Africans, Germans, Finns, Russians and people of many other nationalities have been unforgettable. These warm encounters in the cold have inspired many new thoughts and notions. I hope I have been able to convey some of them in this book.

It was, in some way, the wish to try to place chance at the centre of some sort of system that motivated me to suggest to my friend Yngve Bergqvist, during the autumn of 1990, that we build a large igloo. It would be the first step towards the creation of a community out of the crisp and frozen vitalizing water of the Torne River and the pure, glistening snow.

Yngve Bergqvist, the 'wilderness director', as he is sometimes known, is well aware of the significance meetings between people can have for the development of a community, a business and those who work for it. After many years at sea, Yngve finally came ashore to meet new people and a different culture, far from the great oceans of the world. Jukkasjärvi and Kiruna, 200 kilometres north of the Arctic Circle in Swedish Lapland, became his new harbour.

And, like a busy harbour, Jukkasjärvi has always greeted people from afar. For nearly five centuries the little village has been hosting meetings of various kinds between people from different parts of the world who have gathered here for worship, trade, research and adventure.

Icehotel, the world's biggest igloo, has strengthened, enlivened and developed this old meeting-place, Jukkasjärvi — a meeting-place for people who like to seize the moment that comes crawling at a snail's pace, but vanishes in a flash.

You, too, can seize the moment.

Pär Granlund

10

There are no fewer than eight seasons in Lapland. The transitions between the seasons are also seasons. For the reindeer-herding Sami, every season has a special significance. Time, for the Sami, is marked by the workings of Nature, everyday life and the migration of the herd, not by clocks and calendars. Renrajd, the big drove to grazing-lands or the corral.

Photo: Tomas Utsi

A DECADE IN THE 500-YEAR HISTORY OF JUKKASJÄRVI

Coinciding with the celebration of a new millennium, Icehotel is celebrating the anniversary of an eventful decade. But what is a decade in 500 years or more? Undoubtedly, the past 10 years in the long life of this historic village have been intensive, exciting and noteworthy.

On the scale of five centuries it was but a moment ago that the first igloo, built from the ice of the frozen Torne River, was erected next to the old open-air museum. It seems like yesterday that Yngve Bergqvist rang up to say, **"Now we're building the igloo."** That was in early February 1991.

A DECADE IN THE 500-YEAR HISTORY OF JUKKASJÄRVI

A few days previously Jukkasjärvi had been covered in a deep layer of giant snowflakes. There was more than enough to build an igloo on the metre-thick ice of the river. "Kauko and the others know how," Yngve replied without hesitation a couple of months before that when I asked him whether there was anyone in Jukkasjärvi who could build a large igloo.

For Yngve, the step between thought and action is insignificant. In autumn 1990 I told him of my idea to build an igloo that would be bigger than the well-known structures of the Inuit. A shortage of snow put a stop to those plans, but a few months later the project was in full swing.

The idea was to build an igloo that would manifest the significance of art and culture to an ordered, humane society, an igloo that would also highlight the necessity for people to gather, enjoy one another's company and bridge boundaries of different kinds; an igloo that would take into account the specific conditions of the locality – the history, experience, landscape and climate – was well on its way to becoming a reality. For me, the igloo was much more than a building made of ice and snow. Yngve Bergqvist, the cultural entrepreneur who convinced a little old village on the banks of the Torne River that they, too, could believe in the future, understood this. He understood what was specific to the village in terms of nature, culture, history, traditions and climate.

During the summer of 1990 I had been working on some ideas for the marketing of a family and cultural festival in Piteå, a medium-sized town on the coast of south-eastern Lapland, where the rivers meet the Baltic Sea in the 'bright archipelago'. About 30 of Sweden's foremost artists had been invited to participate in an art project that would attract a lot of media attention and draw a lot of praise from the public. It was midnight. The sun shone brightly as the artists set up their easels to start working on their impressions of the old wooden warehouses situated on the training grounds of the municipal rescue service. Their creative efforts that night resulted in about forty works that later sold for more than SEK 500 000.

Festival-maker Olle Lundqvist's idea was that the annual proceeds should be given, in the

Pär Granlund, free agent and inspirer of the igloo in Jukkasjärvi.

Photo: Per Nilsson, Ateljé Grodan

Yngve Bergqvist, 'wilderness director' of the adventure tourism company Jukkas AB, turned the little igloo into the now world-famous Icehotel. A specific feature of Jukkas AB is that both the company and the villagers offer guests a chance to experience, first-hand, the daily life of the village and its three cultures, Swedish, Finnish and Sami. For anyone who has never experienced winter, snow and cold, drilling into the ice with an ice auger for the first time is an unforgettable experience.

Photo: Peter Grant

form of a grant, to whoever came up with the best ideas for new cultural projects. For him, the festival and the various cultural events also serve as important meeting-places for many different kinds of people, irrespective of age, background or interests. That summer Jan Wikström, an architect and historian from Luleå, was a awarded a grant to help him realise his vision of building a county art gallery. The money proved just enough to keep the idea alive, which, after all, is nonetheless an essential step towards the realisation of any vision.

I continued to carry the idea around in my head and tried persistently to stimulate an interest in the creation of a meeting place – a gallery. Another thought was to create some kind of 'media installation' which would also embody that which is specific to the region – the winter, the ice, the snow and the cold.

The previous winter I had seen an outdoor exhibition involving a number of artists who displayed their works among the high snowdrifts in the central park of Luleå, the principal town of the county. The idea of an ice gallery in ice presented itself as a self-evident and natural element of a winter festival.

An igloo! A big igloo! Bigger than any that had ever been built! Had a large igloo ever, in fact, been built? How is it done? How big can it be? But just as vivid as the idea of an ice gallery were my own doubts. How does one go about building an igloo in the ancient manner of the Inuit?

Roger Lindmark, who at the time was the director of the cold climate research institute Cold Tech at Luleå University, told me of a small igloo built a few years previously by Professor Tsutomu Kokawa from Hokkaido in northern Japan. A research report, "Field Study on Ice Shell", contained charts and diagrams with measurements of structural strength and other important data. The report and statistics were never used. All the knowledge that was needed could be found in Jukkasjärvi, in the experience of Yngve Bergqvist, Kauko Notström and their colleagues.

"The igloo will be big, and beside it there will be smaller igloos for people to stay in, or at least visit for a few hours," I remember saying as I presented my idea to Yngve. The igloo should be like the old church and cottages in Gammelstad outside Luleå. Every winter the igloo will be recreated, in one form or another. The 'ice community' will be a place for people to mingle and

Konstlotsen, a group of artists from Mölle in the southern Swedish county of Scania, showed their work at the igloo ARTic Hall. Visitors had the impression that the paintings were floating in mid-air, thanks to the transparent nylon thread used to suspend the works from the vaulted ceiling.

Photo: Eivon Carlsson

The 500 or so cottages of Gammelstad in Luleå, the principal town in the county, served as inspiration for the first igloo in Jukkasjärvi, built in 1991. Dating from 1492, the Gammelstad church, a gathering place and regional centre of worship, is included in the UNESCO World Heritage list of culturally and historically unique buildings.

Photo: Per Svensson

Built on the ice of the Torne River in February 1991, the first igloo had a floor area of just over 50 square metres. ARTic Hall marked the inception of a new community, a meeting-place created out of the very best ice, 'harvested' from the 700km-long, crystal-clear Torne River.

Photo: Pär Granlund.

have a good time together. There was, and still is, something in common between Jukkasjärvi and the unique cottages of the church village of Gammelstad, now a UNESCO World Heritage site. Both are significant as meeting-places.

In early February, when Yngve rang me up to give the word that building had begun, there was no time for detailed planning. It was simply a matter of taking a quick leap from thought to action. I put down the phone, picked it up again and dialled Jannot Derid, an artist based in Luleå. "Do you have any paintings I can borrow for an exhibition in an ice gallery?"

Momentarily stunned by the oddity of the question, Jannot consented without further ado and promised me several works. When the day arrived we packed 10 paintings carefully into a borrowed van and set off along the 370-kilometre-long ice-covered road to Kiruna and Jukkasjärvi. Five hours later, in the cold of the night, we stopped outside the igloo by the open-air museum. The snow squeaked under our feet as we walked with "bated breath" down towards the igloo. It had taken countless shovels-full of snow and a fair amount of sweaty toil and required the use of a number sturdy wooden beams and chipboard which were used as forms. There was a little door in one side; otherwise, it was just a big, hollow mound of snow. There was really very little difference between this igloo and the small piles of snow I played in as a child on Tingvallsgatan in Malmberget, back in the '50s, although this one was much bigger, of course.

Rumours of the igloo ice gallery circulated among the villagers faster than the Northern Lights across a clear winter sky. More than 500 curious villagers of all ages came walking or kick-sledding to the igloo to see an unusual exhibition of colourful art by Jannot Derid. The works harmonised with the shifting whites and greens and blues of the ice and snow around them.

For many, it was perhaps their first visit to a gallery. The sombre silence that usually reigns over a vernissage never darkened the door of this event. The ice gallery was buzzing with lively chatter. The cold air, the smell of paint and the warmth of the vibrant colours awakened the senses of the onlookers.

"Allah is great today," commented Jannot as we left the gallery for the night and wandered off to our warm cabin. The art gallery and meeting-place ARTic Hall was born.

Pär Granlund

The art teacher and ice sculptor Karin Bergqvist from Jukkasjärvi created a work of art with Sami religious symbols engraved in ice. Several of the symbols are used in the logotype of the adventure tourism company Jukkas AB. *Top left:* the thunder god Horagalles. *Right:* a Sami shaman. *Bottom left:* the wind god Biegolmai. *Right:* Leibomai, god of the hunt. The cross in the middle symbolizes the Sun, Peive.

Photo. Tomas Utsi

On entering the cavernous hall of ice, built at Icehotel in
1996-97, visitors felt as if they were in a fairy-tale world.

Photo: Tomas Utsi

FOREWORD BY YNGVE BERGQVIST

ANYTHING IS POSSIBLE!

Anything is possible! Well, perhaps it is going slightly too far to suggest that there is nothing that could not be achieved in our little village; but with the right idea, a good dose of will-power and ambition, and the right colleagues and partners, a lot is possible.

ANYTHING IS POSSIBLE!

We discovered that it was possible to build the world's largest igloo, complete with a hotel, a beautiful bar called the Absolut Ice Bar, an ice chapel and even an ice sauna. We created all of it, and surrounded it with some of the most beautiful ice art the world has ever seen.

It's all a matter of survival, of trusting in one's ability to make the best use of what is available. History and experience have shown that survival often depends on finding the right partner. For those of us who live and work in Jukkasjärvi, survival also involves a sense of pride in nearly five centuries of history and unique local traditions, as well as in our three co-existing cultures – the Sami, the Finnish and the Swedish. As inhabitants of Jukkasjärvi we are proud of our common culture and heritage. We are proud of the fact that people from all over the world are interested in our village, and want to visit us and become better acquainted with the place we call home.

For several centuries, Jukkasjärvi has been a natural meeting-place – for religious festivals, for trade and commerce. In recent times, the village has attracted adventurers, nature-lovers and people who take an interest in other cultures, as well as many others who simply like to enjoy life and make the most of every moment. Meeting-places for people from different cultures are essential in times such as these, when the dominating form of international communication is electronic. IT is a great way of finding each other in the wide world, but real meetings between people have to take place in special places. On behalf of the people of Jukkasjärvi, I am very pleased to be able to say that our old village is becoming an even more important meeting-place.

The igloo and Best Western Icehotel have become famous throughout the world. This unique building represents our attempt to take advantage of, and develop, that which already exists in abundance in Swedish Lapland: winter, cold, snow and ice. Visitors to the hotel are overwhelmed by the fabulous ice art created by some of the world's finest ice sculptors; but many are also sad that these works of art will be lost forever with the arrival of spring and the bright rays of the Midnight Sun. They forget that the igloo and its art are like life itself: inevitably, all things must one day perish. From this indisputable fact only one sensible conclusion can be drawn. Seize the day and make the most of every moment! Live by this motto and you will find that, even in the short scope of a human life, it is possible to realize just about anything.

Yngve Bergqvist
Manager, Jukkas AB

The ice obelisk at Icehotel is more than 15 metres tall and 3 metres thick. A pump placed on top floods the obelisk with pure Torne River water. Climbers use the obelisk to practice their technique.

Photo: Tomas Utsi

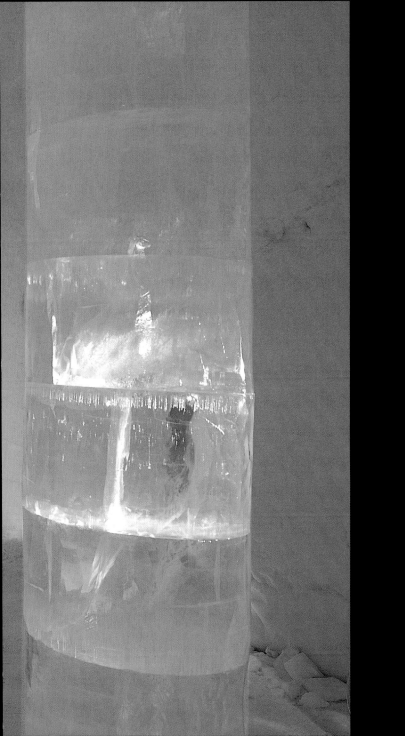

It's always a pleasure to sit back in comfort in one of the ice armchairs of the hotel lobby. Who will be arriving tonight?

Photo: Tomas Utsi

THERE´S NO BUSINESS LIKE SNOWBUSINESS!

Steel, paper, iron ore, hydro power and forestry products have long been the major exports of Norrbotten and Lapland in northern Sweden.

When Icehotel was created, the region and Sweden were given something new to offer the world – experiences – like sleeping in an igloo, enjoying a cold drink in the ice bar, looking at ice art or even getting married in the ice chapel.

THERE´S NO BUSINESS LIKE SNOWBUSINESS!

The fact that there is a large igloo in Jukkasjärvi is something that few people can have failed to notice. Newspapers, radio and and television around the world have produced vivid reports of the unique building on the banks of the Torne River. Each year since February 1991 the adventure company Jukkas AB and, later, Icehotel AB, have been building the world's biggest igloo.

For every year the igloo has grown bigger and more magnificent. The first version had a floor area of a mere 50 square metres. But this only confirms the old Chinese proverb: 'even a thousand-mile journey begins with a single step'. The interior of the igloo and its artistic decoration have also evolved over the years. No ice suite or other room is, or ever has been, the same as any other. Naturally, the ice artists wish to put their own distinctive touch on the suites they decorate.

"We often receive inquiries from artists and architects who would like to come and work in Jukkasjärvi," explains Yngve Bergqvist.

Work on the igloo begins in November when the temperature has dropped to about -2°C to -3°C (about 27°-28° Fahrenheit). High-quality artificial snow is sprayed over large sheet-metal building forms. When the snow has become as hard as ice the forms are removed.

The 1998-99 Icehotel was completed in only 38 days. As the construction technique is developed and Icehotel recruits more ice builders, the igloo can materialize in even less time. A new freezer building with a 1,500-tonne capacity will supply the necessary ice.

Thousands of tonnes of ice are needed to build an igloo. Cutting blocks of ice from the river and fitting them together can be difficult and hazardous. But no one has yet been injured while working with the heavy blocks of ice. This is because the builders are experienced and have developed a sense of judgement and an eye for safety.

Many of the visitors to the ice hotel in Jukkasjärvi are business people who want to treat their clients and colleagues to an unusual and unforgettable experience which can also be a good way of bonding and strengthening personal relationships. Conferences and meetings are interspersed with snowmobiling and wilderness excursions with the professional sled-dog driver Kenth Fjellborg and his team of eager Huskies.

Fjällräven, a Swedish outdoor clothing manufacturer, commissioned the ice artist
Karin Bergqvist to create an ice statue of the company's well-known symbol, the arctic fox.

Photo: Tomas Utsi

Relaxing with a good book in an ice suite. Guests sleep comfortably in specially-made sleeping-bags which stay warm and cosy down to **-35°C (-31° Fahrenheit)**. Under the sleeping-bag is a warm layer of warm reindeer hides. The temperature inside the igloo varies between -6°C and -9°C (18°F to 21°F).

The art on the wall above the bed was created by the well-known veteran ice and snow artist Albert Falck from Gällivare. His motifs were inspired by the farming and forestry traditions of northern Sweden.

Photo: Tomas Utsi

Newsweek ranked Absolut Icebar among the world's 15 most unique bars. Ice artists first made a giant Absolut bottle of ice in 1996.

Photo: Tomas Utsi

"We are starting to get more visits from private individuals and smaller groups of people, so we are building additional smaller ice suites to accommodate them," explains Yngve Bergqvist.

Rest assured, there's no chance of freezing to death in the igloo. In specially made Fjällräven sleeping-bags that stay warm and cosy down to -35°C (-31° Fahrenheit), guests enjoy a pleasant arctic night's sleep on ice block beds that are clad in reindeer hides. Temperatures inside the igloo are relatively constant, remaining at -6°C to -9°C (18 to 21° Fahrenheit) while outdoors, the mercury drops to -25°C (-13°F). A delightful night's rest in one of Icehotel's enchanting ice suites is followed by a steamy sauna and hearty breakfast at the inn.

One of Icehotel's many partners, Absolut, the popular vodka brand, showed an interest early on to take advantage of the positive values represented by the igloo – its purity and clarity. Initially, the company commissioned a unique ice bar, an obvious feature of which was Absolut's characteristic vodka bottle – the packaging for one of Sweden's most successful export products. Today, the large version and the smaller versions can be seen in the igloo.

Absolut also brought in a number of famous fashion models, including Naomi Campbell, Kate Moss and Marcus Schenkenberg, for some chilly shoots inside the igloo. Gianni Versace, the fashion designer, was also invited by Absolut to create a special collection – a free interpretation of the Absolut Vodka trademark. The collection comprised an exciting blend of elegant evening wear and leisurewear. The ice artists Arne Bergh and Åke Larsson sculpted an ornamental Medusa head (Versace's symbol) in ice to frame the face of Kate Moss. Wearing ice wigs designed by Danilo Dixon, the models resembled mystical ice goddesses.

The results of the models' and the internationally acclaimed photographer Herb Ritts's -30°C shoot appeared in eight million copies of a supplement to Vogue, one of the world's most respected fashion magazines.

TV companies, radio stations and newspapers throughout the world got wind of the shoot in Jukkasjärvi. An estimated 600 million people have seen the pictures of the models among the works of ice art. The publicity focussed massive worldwide attention on Icehotel, which gained further exposure when Naomi Campbell intimated in an interview that she had practically frozen to death in Jukkasjärvi.

The appropriately named Crystal Room (Kristallrummet), designed by the artist Åke Larsson. The room contains a topographic negative relief map of Tornedalen's rivers and valleys along the border with Finland. The map can be viewed in animated form at Icehotel's website, *www.icehotel.com.*

Photo: Tomas Utsi

A dream world! A fantasy world! A fairy-tale world!

Photo: Peter Grant

"It was great marketing for us, since we target people who want to experience winter, snow and cold in a unique and exotic natural and cultural environment," says Yngve Bergqvist, who is convinced that anything is possible given a bright idea and the right partners.

Another project that drew attention to Icehotel was the shooting of the Danish film director Billy August's *Smilla's Sense of Snow*. The ice architect and artist Arne Bergh designed an artificial glacier for the set. A full account of all the fascinating events, arrangements and happenings, great and small, which have taken place at Icehotel would be both long and impressive.

Yngve Bergkvist and his colleagues were the first in Sweden to take tourists and others white-water rafting on the Torne River, and to arrange every imaginable form of sauna bathing. The adventure tourism industry in Jukkasjärvi went professional in a big way in the early '80s. The efforts of Bergkvist and his colleagues have earned them several awards and honours, including the "Liseberg Applause" and "Werner of the Year" awards, for the inn's superb cuisine. Sweden's state tourism delegation acknowledged the work of Yngve Bergqvist in 1994 by awarding him the prestigious Stora turismpriset. The jury motivated its decision as follows:

"By utilising local conditions, Yngve Bergqvist has built up a tourism industry that has gained wide recognition outside the country. Each year, out of about 85,000 guests, half are from abroad, including many from Germany, Great Britain, France and Japan. The hotel offers a number of truly Swedish adventure activities, such as dog-sledding, white-water rafting, helicopter excursions, fishing, hotel accommodation in an igloo and, more recently, the spectacular ARTic Hall. In Jukkasjärvi, the principle of encouraging creativity and supporting local initiatives to start new sub-contracting businesses has had a positive effect on tourism in the area and throughout Norrbotten."

"Adventure tourism in Jukkasjärvi is a uniquely Swedish export product," says Bergqvist. "We do our marketing and selling abroad, but the product is consumed here, in our own country. 65 per cent of our guests come from abroad."

Photo: Tomas Utsi

Jukkas AB's business concept is to develop and arrange stimulating and memorable wilderness adventures for guests who are looking for genuine, high-quality outdoor adventure activities and close interaction with nature. The activities are based on a relationship of trust and confidence between guests and staff.

The company's key assets are its well-trained and attentive staff, good communications and close links with local culture. The company strives to ensure that all guests are completely satisfied with their experiences in the village and surrounding area. To achieve this goal the company operates year-round, offering a programme of attractive activities for every season. Other objectives are to maintain a good level of return 12 months of the year, and for staff to feel a sense of pride and status in working for Jukkas AB.

The first igloo in Jukkasjärvi, built in 1991, was not, in fact, the first 'ice product' from Jukkas AB. In late November 1989 a symposium, focusing on how winter and ice could be used to advantage, was held. The participants included artists from Sweden and the highly-acclaimed ice sculptors Sadao Ogi and Keiichi Oso from Ashaikawa, Japan. One of the initiators of the symposium and workshop was Rune Sundmark, then president of the national organization for ice and snow sculptors, which is based in Kiruna.

"We're very grateful for his efforts," says Yngve Bergqvist. "He was the one who secured the resources required to hold the symposium".

Rune Sundmark is a creative, enthusiastic individual who has grasped the importance of continuous professional development. He is responsible for laying the foundations of and developing ice art in the region and the rest of Sweden. Per-Erik Svensson, formerly an official at the regional development department of the County Administration, secured a grant of 20,000 kronor for the arrangers to cover the Japanese artists' travel costs. The Swedish Board of Tourism, the National Arts Council, the Municipality of Kiruna and City of Ashaikawa also provided funding.

"We went to the old church in Jukkasjärvi by kick-sled. The sky was blood-red," Rune Sundmark recalls. "The weekend took a dramatic turn when Kiruna was surprised by warm winds during the night. It was as if someone had taken a blow torch to the sculptures. The Japanese artists' reindeer and eagle were destroyed, and the big Lapp tent blew all the way to Vittangi. But the symposium continued, despite the weather conditions, and the valiant ice artists displayed their talent and craft by sculpting new works the following day. We are very grateful to these artists and the city of Ashaikawa. All ended well, and the sequel was particularly successful, thanks to you people up in Jukkasjärvi".

It is never easy to foretell future events, but we hope, on entering a new millennium, that 500-year-old Jukkasjärvi and the decade-old Icehotel still have many exciting and eventful years ahead of them. Thousands of people from a wide range of countries have already visited Icehotel. They may have spent a night in the igloo, perhaps several, and they have experienced much of what the old village and the surrounding low woodland wilderness have to offer. Upon returning home, the visitors tell of their experiences, and their encounter with ice art. Their positive impressions are passed on to friends and relatives whose curiosity is aroused. Perhaps they, too, will some day make the pilgrimage to the fabulous place in the far north.

In addition to the traditional export products of Norrbotten, Lapland and the rest of Sweden, there is now a new, well-established export product from Jukkasjärvi. As the villagers are wont to say: *"There's no business like snow business!"*

At the ice bar, not only do you get ice in your drink, you get your drink in ice. Each year, thousands of handmade ice glasses are produced. Mother Nature does the washing up, or rather, recycling. Production of new glasses starts again in November.

Photo: Peter Grant

Many a guest has wondered, **"But that big crystal chandelier must surely be real?"** Indeed it is. Every detail is made of crystal-clear ice.

Photo: Tomas Utsi

Åke Larsson worked in wood before discovering the mystique
of ice. A cool encounter one frosty night in January converted him.

Photo: Peter Grant

Representatives from Greenland Tourism, Hanseeraq and Fartato, have visited
Icehotel to learn how to build an igloo. A number of Greenland adventure
tourism companies are now planning to build a Santa Igloo Village. The project
is part of a major initiative to develop the winter tourism industry.

Photo: Peter Grant

ICECHURCH

Your gift of love, Your beauty,
in winter now abiding.
Your great wealth of love
I will bestow upon the
frosted trees and the autumn
seeds that sleep in the earth,
in God's winter in the North.

No. 861 from
Psalmer i 90-talet
(Psalms for the '90s)

Photo: Tomas Utsi
Ice sculptor: Barbro Behm

After 25 years as an art teacher in Kiruna, Barbro Behm decided to go into the culture business on her own. Her ice art in the Ice Church next to the hotel is one of her many internationally acclaimed creations.

Barbro explains the idea behind her company, Ice Pol Art: "I have always loved winter and I want people to be able to see and appreciate the fantastic possibilities this season, snow and ice have to offer."

ICECHURCH

Five years of study at an art school in Chicago contributed a great deal to her artistic and personal development. At the age of 18 she left the small town of Kalix, where the river meets the sea and the bright archipelago of Norrbotten and Lapland. That was in 1962. Barbro went over to the big country in the west, where she stayed with an émigré uncle.

"America is a tough country to live in, but it is also a country of tremendous opportunities. Anyone who has the ideas, and the ambition to realise them, can succeed. Americans have a positive and appreciative attitude to people who have some talent, work hard and want to achieve something." While on holiday in Sweden she met the love of her life. Her return ticket to the States was never used. Instead of a career as an artist in the United States, Barbro continued her studies at an arts college in Stockholm, then worked in advertising for a few years.

In the mid-'70s she and her husband Jan moved to Vittangi, where she had been offered a job as a teacher. Alongside her day job Barbro continued to work on her art. Her ambition as an art teacher and artist has always been to encourage viewers of art to recognize and acknowledge their emotions, what they feel towards an image.

"Many people say they don't understand art, but it isn't a matter of comprehension. It's all about opening your senses, removing the blinkers, using your imagination and allowing yourself to feel something. What matters is that you are moved and that you listen to your own emotions," she explains. For Barbro, life and the stages on which it takes place are all part of one big, living yet transitory, work of art. That is one of the reasons why she loves the winter so much.

"I get a fantastic feeling every time the first snowflakes whiten the ground. It gives me new strength. The fatigue I sometimes experience during the summer disappears during the winter".

In the mid-'80s she was invited to take part in a snow-sculpture competition as part of a new snow festival in Kiruna. It was this event that launched her career as an ice artist of international repute, and she went on to score new successes in competitions in China, Russia, Finland, Italy, Japan, the United States and Norway.

"Back then, certain people looked down their noses at snow art. They didn't think adults should be playing around with snow. Fortunately, that kind of intolerance no longer exists".

Is it right for the Church to be involved in a commercial activity, such as Icehotel? What message does the Church have for those who visit the igloo? These questions have been discussed in ecclesiastical circles, even at a conference of the clergy in Jukkasjärvi. "It is within the context of tourism that the Ice Church finds its principal role and function, and its future," Jan-Erik Johansson, the vicar of Jukkasjärvi Parish, argued during the conference. "The Ice Church has a natural place in the activities conducted by Jukkas AB for tourists and visitors".

Even the parishioners use the church as they would their own. The Ice Church, which is a gift from Icehotel to the parish, was consecrated on Saturday, 28 March 1992.

Photo: Tomas Utsi

The font is filled with pure, life-giving water from the Torne River. The font was designed by the internationally acclaimed ice artist Barbro Behm, who also decorated the interior of the church.

The ice church is a meeting place for people who happen to be in the area. In relation to the village church, the ice church lives a life of its own.

"There is little comparison between the two great churches," says Jan-Erik Johansson, the vicar. It is a place where people can gather to experience fellowship and human warmth. In a temporary structure there is little time for long-winded speeches and dogmatic subtleties. Here, it is a matter of dealing with uncertainty and discussing the crucial aspects of life."

Photo: Tomas Utsi

Barbro Behm is one of the world's foremost ice sculptors. She has taught art for 25 years in Kiruna and now works independently as an artist. Her commissions include the interior of the ice church. "Working with ice is a challenge, since the material very often decides the outcome, and the colours don't always turn out the same." Ice is hard, brittle – and unpredictable.

Photo: Kenneth Paulsson

The big ice festival in Kiruna, ice sculpture courses, Barbro Behm's world championship awards, Icehotel and the Ice Church have all made a strong contribution to raising the status of winter art. Barbro travels around Sweden to hold courses for aspiring snow and ice artists. She arranges competitions and ice-sculpting events, where she creates her sculptures in front of crowds of spectators. Together with her French colleague Colette Cossin, she created a sculpture at the Place du Allees in Paris for a European fresh water conference. Since 1992 she has been commissioned by the parish of Jukkasjärvi to decorate the Ice church near Icehotel. Just like the hotel, the church takes on a new appearance each year.

"I have a basic concept for creating the church interior," she explains. "The church has certain features that are always necessary, for example an altar and a font." The vicar of Jukkasjärvi Parish, Jan-Erik Johansson, is also a trained artist, and he supports Barbro Behm fully in her work.

"I want those who visit the church to be able to feel warmth from the snow and ice. My colleague, Albert Falck, has really succeeded in creating a sense of warmth in the rooms he has decorated at Icehotel. The guests experience a fantastic feeling of warmth upon entering their rooms. Even though she generally has a clear idea of what she wants to create from the blocks of ice, which vary in size and shape, she remains open to what the character of the ice itself suggests. Ice can be both hard and capricious.

"If there is a crack, or a lot of air bubbles, I try to incorporate that into the piece. It's my way of revealing the inherent possibilities of ice to the viewer." The tranquillity and spiritual calm that permeates the church is conducive to a moment of quiet reflection.

"It allows you to free yourself from all that is inessential in life," Barbro Behm comments. Although the ice is transitory and fleeting, it also conveys something of the eternal. In the ice church you are so tangibly enveloped by winter. The church only exists for a very limited period of time. It is therefore not afflicted with the various problems that can arise in conventional buildings. You leave the ice church with a positive feeling that stays with you for a long time. Barbro remembers a woman from the south who visited Jukkasjärvi for a few days in deep winter.

"She went into the chapel several times and just sat there quietly, on her own. For her, just sitting in quiet contemplation was a wonderful experience". The silence is intensified because the ice walls of the church keep out any sound. The ice church serves the same purpose as a conventional church. Services, weddings and christenings are common. Swedish Television's 'Evening Prayer' has also broadcast one of its programmes from the church.

Christenings and weddings in the ice church have become increasingly popular. By 1998, after six years of existence, 51 children had been christened in the ice church by the parish vicar, Jan-Erik Johansson. During the same time 52 couples had been wedded there and hundreds of thousands of people had visited the church.

Photo: Eivon Carlsson, Ice sculptor: Barbro Behm

"**I want those who visit the church to be able to feel warmth from the snow and ice.** My colleague, Albert Falck, has really succeeded in creating a sense of warmth in the rooms he has decorated at Icehotel. The guests experience a fantastic feeling of warmth upon entering their rooms.

Barbro Behm

Photo: Eivon Carlsson

THE SNOW MUST GO ON!

"What are the limits of ice? Where do we draw the boundary between what can and cannot be made from it? This underlying challenge is what inspires us to work with ice," say Åke Larsson and Arne Bergh, the architects of a unique structure built anew out of ice every year. Both are wood artists who became ice converts after a visit to Jukkasjärvi.

THE SNOW MUST GO ON!

Originally from Kiruna, Åke Larsson has lived and worked as an artist in the old university town of Uppsala, north of the Swedish capital, Stockholm. Wood was always his main medium. Until he visited Icehotel in 1993.

"My first visit to the hotel affected me deeply. It was about four in the afternoon, one day in late January," Åke recalls. It was -30°C (-22°F). Like two dark silhouettes against the colourful northern sky, two figures were labouring outside the igloo in defiance of the bitter cold. They were busy cutting two huge blocks of ice with special tools.

"Above all, it was the sound of ice being cut away, and the tinkling sound as it hit the ground, that had such an impact on me. Poetic! Then I saw Tomas Utsi's multi-image presentation and it brought tears of longing to my eyes for the lost winters of my childhood. I felt an overwhelming desire to begin working in ice. A piece of paper I read – someone's vision to create a whole town of snow and ice – gave me a kick. Thoughts of transforming the snow-fort into an ice palace took hold of my mind. The bit of paper which I still have, and read from time to time, has been a source of inspiration to me. That vision was far from what I saw the first time, but it was something I definitely wanted to be a part of."

In Uppsala he had collaborated with Arne Bergh, who also worked in wood. Both have earned a considerable reputation for their work in this medium, and are represented in a number of galleries and public places around Sweden.

Arne Bergh, born in Skövde in central Sweden, spent part of his youth in the garrison town of Boden, in Norrbotten. Arne trained to be an artist at an art college in Stockholm and settled down to work from a studio in Uppsala. His commissions include wood sculptures for the Wasa Museum in Stockholm and the Swedish pavilion at the 1992 world expo in Seville in 1992. In the mid-'90s, neither he nor his friend Åke had the faintest idea of what awaited them in another, colder part of the world. Åke asked Arne to accompany him to his boyhood Kiruna, to take part in the annual snow festival which is held in late January.

"At the time, we knew practically nothing about Jukkas and Icehotel, but we went anyway," Arne recalls.

Not even the thick, hard walls of Icehotel can stop the King of the Forest, the moose. Albert Falk is a well-known and respected name among ice and snow artists throughout the world.

Photo: Eivon Carlsson

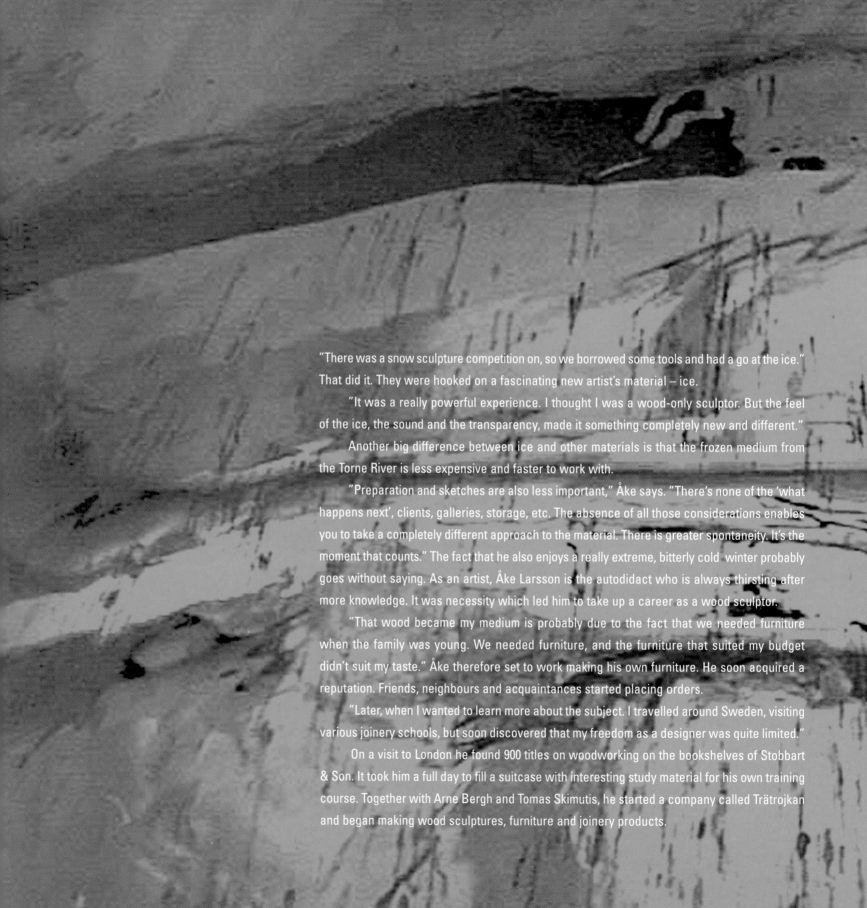

"There was a snow sculpture competition on, so we borrowed some tools and had a go at the ice." That did it. They were hooked on a fascinating new artist's material – ice.

"It was a really powerful experience. I thought I was a wood-only sculptor. But the feel of the ice, the sound and the transparency, made it something completely new and different."

Another big difference between ice and other materials is that the frozen medium from the Torne River is less expensive and faster to work with.

"Preparation and sketches are also less important," Åke says. "There's none of the 'what happens next', clients, galleries, storage, etc. The absence of all those considerations enables you to take a completely different approach to the material. There is greater spontaneity. It's the moment that counts." The fact that he also enjoys a really extreme, bitterly cold winter probably goes without saying. As an artist, Åke Larsson is the autodidact who is always thirsting after more knowledge. It was necessity which led him to take up a career as a wood sculptor.

"That wood became my medium is probably due to the fact that we needed furniture when the family was young. We needed furniture, and the furniture that suited my budget didn't suit my taste." Åke therefore set to work making his own furniture. He soon acquired a reputation. Friends, neighbours and acquaintances started placing orders.

"Later, when I wanted to learn more about the subject. I travelled around Sweden, visiting various joinery schools, but soon discovered that my freedom as a designer was quite limited."

On a visit to London he found 900 titles on woodworking on the bookshelves of Stobbart & Son. It took him a full day to fill a suitcase with interesting study material for his own training course. Together with Arne Bergh and Tomas Skimutis, he started a company called Trätrojkan and began making wood sculptures, furniture and joinery products.

Ice sculptors:
Sadao Ogi, Keiichi Ohsio

In the late 1980s Jukkas AB arranged a training course for ice artists from all over Sweden together with the local labour exchange, the County Labour Board and the Swedish Ice and Snow Sculpture Association. The instructors, Sadao Ogi and Keiichi Oso, demonstrated their amazing talents by creating fabulous works of art. Those November days in Jukkasjärvi were windy and wet; it was above zero.

Photo: Tomas Utsi

Who was the man who turned up at Icehotel
one cold winter's day with his companion?
Perhaps the ice artist Barbro Behm knows.

Photo: Tomas Utsi

"Eventually my furniture started to take on more of a sculptural character, and when I realized that form had started to surpass function I threw away the order book and cancelled all the orders," Åke explains.

"When Arne and I visited Icehotel and discovered that not even durability could prevail over form, we realized that we had found our material."

Their presence, and their commitment to the Icehotel project, have given the igloo a definite boost. With their strong, skilled hands and an abundance of creativity, these two visionary ice artists have further enhanced the style and beauty of Icehotel. Their work on Icehotel takes up all their time, which means that they are unable to attend the many national and international ice sculpture contests that are held annually. Even as the last drops of Icehotel seep back to Mother Earth they already have to start working on the design of next year's igloo. The shapes emerge out of the artists' own creative ambitions and are developed on a computer with the help of design programs.

Their experience from creating the ice art for Herb Ritts's pictures of Naomi Campbell and others, the artificial glacier for the shooting of Billy August's *Smilla's Sense of Snow* and the Ice Pavilion in Stockholm, as well as a long row of other works of ice art for export have led them to ask themselves: what are the limits of ice art?

But building Icehotel requires more than artistic talent and a large amount of ice. Arne Bergh and Åke Larsson stress the importance of the technical requirements, for example, the

The inspiration for the Japanese ice swan came to Renée
Maas during a visit to Jukkasjärvi. Maas later arranged a show
in Groningen, with 1,000 tonnes of Torne River ice art created by
18 Chinese artists.

Photo: Tomas Utsi

equipment needed to drill and cut the ice. Together with Gunnar Andersson from Malmberget,
a small mining community 120km south of Kiruna, they have developed new technologies for
working the ice.

"We describe the function of the machines and Gunnar makes them," Åke Larsson
explains. "Together we've developed methods for determining the optimum milling speed of
chainsaws for ice and snow. The machine for pillar blocks has changed the way we build.
Without it, we could never have built these long halls or the big ice walls outside Gunnar's
sawing station."

Their reward for their work on Icehotel is the appreciative response from the guests and the
spirit of optimism among those who struggle against time and the elements in Jukkasjärvi that they
have helped to engender.

"All water is part of an ecological cycle. To work with ice from a river – running water
whose course is arrested for six months of the year; to see the change, the spring thaw, and
its return to the river and the sea...," Arne Bergh muses as he speaks of his and his colleague
Åke Larsson's role, and that of their crystal-clear ice art, in the greater scheme of things.

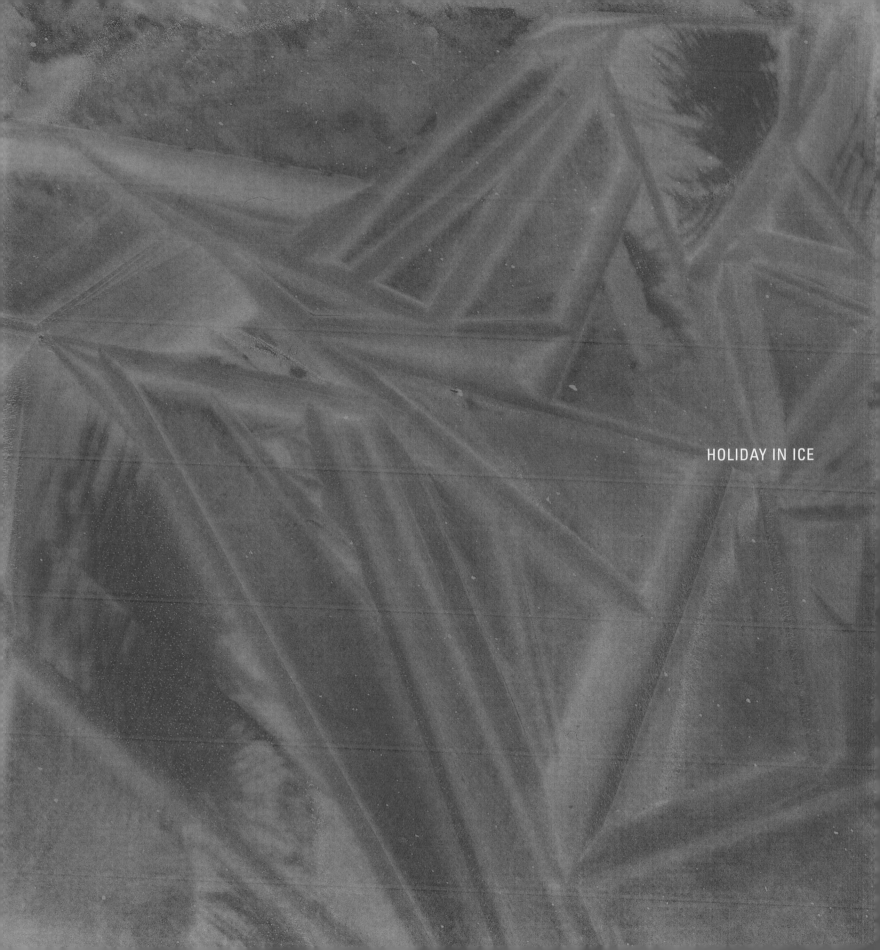

HOLIDAY IN ICE

It is difficult for those who have never visited Icehotel to conjure up an image of its interior. Even the most vivid imagination is unable to paint an inner picture of this magical edifice of ice.

Photo: Peter Grant

The Northern Lights have always fascinated people, even frightening them at a time when little was known about this amazing phenomenon. The best time to see the Northern Lights swirling in colourful veils or flaming up in the sky is on cold evenings when the skies are perfectly clear. Aurora borealis, the Northern Lights, is Nature's show of coloured light in the winter skies of the northern regions of the world. A similar phenomenon, which appears across the polar regions of the southern hemisphere, is known as the aurora australis, the Southern Lights. The auroras are named after the Roman goddess of dawn. The Latin names were first used to describe the phenomena in the early 1600s.

The Sami also have a name for the phenomenon – guovsahas – 'audible light.' Researchers in Kiruna have been studying the auroras since 1957, and it is now known what causes them. Very briefly, a fast stream of charged particles originating in the Sun collides with gas molecules in the upper atmosphere of the earth, causing the emission of visible light. The particles are attracted to the polar regions due to the magnetic influence of the earth. You can learn more about the Northern Lights by visiting: http://www.irf.se

Photo: Torbjörn Lövgren

Guests sleep comfortably in an ice suite after a full day of exciting activities in the sub-arctic cold. Jukkasjärvi's local transit fleet, i.e., a few kick-sleds, illuminated by the clear, moonlit boreal sky.

Photo: Tomas Utsi

Aurora borealis, the Northern Lights, is called the "audible light" by the Sami because of the crackling sound which is said to be heard when the lights appear. Researchers in Kiruna have been studying the phenomenon, which has become an area of extensive scientific interest, since 1957. Space physicists and environmental researchers from around the world come to Kiruna to study the heavens from ground level and with the help of satellite images. A more intimate knowledge of space helps us to understand our own, terrestrial environment. In Salmijärvi, near Jukkasjärvi, the European Space Agency (ESA) has set up a satellite station in the wilderness of the Talma Sami reserve.

Photo: Tomas Utsi

The light in Jukkasjärvi and Swedish Lapland shifts dramatically during the 'Eight Seasons' of the year. It is early March, and the rays of the coming Midnight Sun are growing stronger every day. King Bore, who reigns over winter, has left his throne of ice.

Photo: Tomas Utsi

Icehotel even caters to film buffs. Film and multi-image presentations on nature and the environment are projected directly onto the icy wall of the cinema. Snow crystals sparkle in the light of the projectors.

Photo: Tomas Utsi

82

Photo: Eivon Carlsson

Known as the Vodka King, Lars Olof Smith began industrial-scale distillation of his Absolut Rent Brännvin (Absolutely Pure Spirits) in Sweden in the late 1800s. Vodka and other types of grain alcohol have long been produced in Sweden, but it was not until the late 20th century that state-owned Vin & Sprit made Swedish vodka a popular product on international markets. The Absolut bottle is graced by a portrait of Lars Olof Smith. The ice artist Arne Bergh did a rendition of the portrait on an ice bottle.

Photo: Tomas Utsi

To bring more light into Icehotel, two side walls were built in ice on the east and west sides, respectively. Even if the Sun is not visible during the darkest months, it is never really dark in Jukkasjärvi and Lapland, because the snow, which shifts between white and soft shades of blue, reflects and magnifies the light.

Photo: Tomas Utsi

Thrilling experiences in Lapland's unique wilderness are just part of what Jukkas AB offers guests from all around the world. A snowmobile trip to a hut in the woods is one of many popular adventures. "We try to minimize the impact on nature in a number of ways," says Mikael Jernelöf, the sports manager of the adventure tourism company.

To reduce exhaust emissions from snowmobiles, so-called PFI systems have been installed. Jukkas AB's policy is to reduce environmental impact wherever technically and economically possible.

Photo: Tomas Utsi

Jukkasjärvi offers countless possibilities for viewing the natural world from a variety of perspectives. Jan Toreheim, from the Absolut Company, stood on his head during the official opening of the ice bar, even managing to drink a toast in that position. The ice and snow sculptress Lena Kriström recreated the moment.

Photo: Tomas Utsi

Ice sculptor: Helena Rosang

Formerly an assistant nurse, Helena Rosang became an ice artist. The impressive horse she made while training for her new profession delighted this little girl from France.

Photo: Tomas Utsi

An encounter with winter, snow and ice can transform adults into playful children.
When that happens, anything goes! The slide is 'polished' frequently. The younger
children have to wait their turn.

Photo: Tomas Utsi

The igloo is normally the scene of a lot of fun and laughter, but the official opening of Icehotel's ice sauna occasioned more celebration than usual. The world-leading sauna maker Tylö from Halmstad in southern Sweden installed the sauna heater in the igloo.

A hotel without a good sauna is no real hotel, and since Icehotel is a real hotel it has a sauna, complete with an adjoining relaxation room. **The Swedish Sauna Academy** was founded in Jukkasjärvi in 1988. The ice sauna is Icehotel's contribution to the promotion and development of sauna culture.

Photo: Kenneth Paulsson

The fashion magazine Vogue did a feature with ice walls and ice furniture as a setting for a photo shoot of models in bathing suits. The article didn't mention whether the models concluded the sweaty session with a refreshing dip in the Torne River.

Photo: Kenneth Paulsson

Woo-Bock Lee, an artist from South Korea, displayed her work at Icehotel. She was so fascinated and inspired by the limitless(?) possibilities of ice that she designed the interior of one of the hotel's suites.

Photo: Kenneth Paulsson

THE ULTIMATE EXPERIENCE

THE ULTIMATE EXPERIENCE

"Icehotel is perhaps the Swedish phenomenon that is most often mentioned by leading American opinion-makers in our discussions with them. A surprising number of them have been there, or are planning a visit, in many cases as their prime reason for visiting Sweden," writes Dag Sebastian Ahlander, Consul-General in New York, in a letter to Jukkas AB. He points out that what many people in Sweden consider a drawback for development, i.e., ice, darkness and cold, can be turned to advantage.

"Behind it all lies the post-modern individual's yearning for new experiences – something off the beaten track. In that sense, Jukkasjärvi is the ultimate experience."

ABOUT JUKKASJÄRVI

- Since the mid-1800s the village has been the home of a religious sect which belongs to the Church of Sweden. The movement was founded by the revivalist preacher Lars Levi Laestadius and bears his name.

- An altar painting in the church depicts the life of Laestadius and his work in Tornedalen. Painted by Bror Hjorth, a well-known Swedish artist, it was commissioned by the mining company LKAB and donated to the parish in 1958.

- About 800 people live in Jukkasjärvi. Many of the villagers are retired; others work for the local council, the county administration, at the space research centre, for the mining company LKAB, or in the private service sector.

- Jukkasjärvi and Icehotel are 17 kilometres from Kiruna's town centre and 9 kilometres from Kiruna Airport.

Photo: Kai Piippo

One of the very first buildings to be erected in Jukkasjärvi in the early 1600s is still standing. On a peninsula near the shores of the Torne River stands a little wooden church, built in 1607 at the initiative of the "King of the Laplanders," Charles IX of Sweden. Ever since the construction of the church, Jukkasjärvi has been an important venue for religious gatherings, as well as for trade, and for experiences; in the broadest sense, of history and nature, and of the unique culture and environment of the village. The name Jukkasjärvi is Finnish and means 'lake of meetings.

Photo: Tomas

According to the rules of golf, the game may only be interrupted in the event of lightning and thunder. A dedicated golfer plays the game year-round, regardless of weather. Outside Icehotel, on the white course of the Torne River, about 40 golfers are taking part in a competition.

Photo: Eivon Carlsson

All ice artists want to set their own distinctive mark on the ice suites they decorate.
Each is unique. How many of the world's hotels undergo such transformation?

Photo: Kai Piippo

Every year in December, Sweden celebrates the memory of the patron saint of Siracusa, Saint Lucia, who died a martyr in AD 304. The red sash symbolizes Lucia's blood.

The tradition was originally brought to Sweden via Germany. It caught on in 1927 when a Stockholm daily paper sponsored a contest to select a Lucia. Today, in schools and communities throughout the country, Lucias are chosen during the weeks before Dec. 13. In Jukkasjärvi, the Lucia procession visits Icehotel.

Photo: Peter Grant

Each winter, the 'ice farm' of the Torne River produces a good crop of the world's best ice. Thousands of tonnes of pure, crystal-clear ice is harvested for use as building material, for interior decoration, and for ice art. Removing snow from the surface of the ice encourages it to accumulate to the desired thickness. Special kinds of ice are required for the various parts of the igloo. Ice art, for example, is made from ice with a higher oxygen content, and ice taken near the shore is dense, which makes it suitable for use in pillars. The perfect temperature for harvesting ice is -10°C (14°F). At colder temperatures, it tends to crack.

Photo: Tomas Utsi

Suddenly, ice appeared in the desert. In an international fashion event staged by the African designer Alphadi in November 1998, the 700 participants were the being frizzled by the scorching sun in the dry and dusty desert of Niger. Cooling relief came in a container from Jukkasjärvi in the form of **12 tonnes** of crystal-clear ice. "Those were the 50 most intensive hours of my life," says the artists Arne Bergh, summing up his efforts to create a work of ice art under the relentless Sun while scores of designers and fashion journalists looked on in wide-eyed amazement. It was the first time there had ever been ice in the desert outside Agadez. And it isn't likely there will will ever be 12 tonnes of ice among the sand dunes again.

When Alphadi, or the desert prince, as he is known, gathered his colleagues from around the world, he wanted to give them a surprise. He succeeded. One of the main sponsors, The Absolut Company, unveiled the event's refreshing big surprise when the mercury hit **35°C (95°F)**. "The ice survived the journey in perfect condition. It was the same when it arrived in Niger as it was when it left Jukkas!" Maersk, who transported the ice, did a fantastic job. They deserve a standing ovation.

Photo: Christophe Lapetit

Arne Bergh, ice artist and part-owner of Icehotel contacted the lighting designer Kai Piippo at the suggestion of a friend in the lighting business. Kai came to work at the igloo.

"Icehotel is the most fascinating locale I have worked in. It's a wonderful milieu, in terms of illumination. Long periods with little or no daylight; and this fabulous structure, with its ice-pillar halls and beautifully decorated suites, each one with an individual character." He says that the makers of Icehotel have managed to create an atmosphere which fosters creativity, in which it is inspiring and rewarding to work.

"My basic ideas for lighting design in this setting are based on contrasts between light and dark, and between hot and cold." Another ambition was to create a magical world inside the hotel without any visible technology. The guests would simply experience the lighting effect. Out with candles and in with concealed electrical lighting. Contrasting darkness and light made the hall of pillars and corridors appear dark, with the only light coming from the walls of ice, and the rooms and suites in the background.

"We were able to achieve a big effect with very little light," explains Kai Piippo. Concealed lights produce a cold glow inside the ice throughout the hotel, in the pillars of the bar, in the walls, even in some of the sculptures. The only warm light is in the guest rooms, which have a cosy feel."

"Another idea was to give the sensation of natural daylight. The public areas are illuminated throughout the day, while in the guest rooms we have created truly magical spaces."

Photo: Kai Piippo

Water – source of life, joy and Icehotel. Use it with care! By June, Icehotel has been transformed into pure water and re-entered the eco-cycle from whence it came, only to be returned to us in November. The 700 km-long Torne River carries crystal-clear water – the source of life, joy and Icehotel.

Photo: Tomas Utsi

THE PHOTOGRAPHERS

Eivon Carlsson

"AT ICEHOTEL, YOU BECOME A CHILD AGAIN."

The photographer Eivon Carlsson has never forsaken Norrbotten and Lapland, but countless pictures taken by this master of the lens have left the region to be published in a variety of magazines and periodicals.

"I live in an incredibly beautiful and unique region," explains Eivon. "There is so much I want to capture and document on film."

When he was barely 11 Eivon was given a complete photo developing kit by his parents. The bathroom soon became a darkroom. His experiments with the camera eventually led to a photography course at a school in Luleå, in 1965. After completing his studies at the age of 18 he began to work as a professional photographer. Based in Luleå, his territory included all of what is known as Nordkalotten (the northernmost regions of Norway, Sweden, Finland and the Kola Peninsula in north-west Russia.) For many years he produced work for daily newspapers and trade magazines in Sweden and abroad. He also produced freelance photo features, which he offered for publication.

His work has been published in many respected journals and periodicals, including National Geographic, Natural History and the Los Angeles Times. Countless readers in England, Germany, Japan and Australia have been amazed by his stunning portrayals of the nature, life and culture of Lapland and Norrbotten. Eivon Carlsson was among the first of his profession to discover the unique structure of ice and snow that is built in Jukkasjärvi in November every year.

Eivon remembers the snow forts of his childhood. "Icehotel is a fascinating building. When you are inside it, you become a child again."

For most of his photojournalism and advertising work, he uses the well-known Swedish Hasselblad (500 series) camera. "Then, there's never any problem," he says. One of the things that has kept Eivon Carlsson in the north is the magical light of the Eight Seasons. For a photographer, this means plenty of opportunities for 'writing with light', as the word photograph, in its original Greek meaning, very aptly suggests.

Peter Grant

"TRAVEL WORK BROUGHT ME TO ICEHOTEL."

Born: 17 March 1965, Wellington, New Zealand

Education: Christ's College, Christchurch, New Zealand, 1978 -1982

Victoria University, 1983-1987, Bachelor of Arts in Sociology and Religious Studies

CAREER

After teaching myself photography and travelling the world I started working as a freelance photojournalist in London, working for small papers and magazines such as The Socialist and The Big Issue, photographing social issues.

My first big break came in 1993, when I shot the Poll Tax riots in Trafalgar Square, and Reuters sold my photographs all around the world.

Working on the streets of London brought me into contact with London's homeless people. For one assignment I moved into a park and lived among them for several months, documenting their lives. This unique access got my photographs into many national papers. I was also working on a documentary entitled Fields Apart, about a homeless community thrown out of an inner London park, which was later broadcast on one of the national television channels in the UK. Eventually my work developed in a more pleasurable direction when I started doing work for skiing and travel publications. It was this travel work that brought me to Icehotel. After seeing my Icehotel photographs in the ski magazine Fall Line, the World of Interiors commissioned me for an Icehotel feature. Interiors has since republished these pictures all over the world in various glamorous publications.

Since 1997 my work has moved in a more commercial direction; for example, annual report photography for companies, organisations and charities.

Publications in which my work has appeared:

1991-1996:
Melody Maker
Time Out
The Guardian
The Independent
Saturday Times
1996-1999
Fall Line
Onboard
TNT
Outdoors Pursuits
Adrenalin

Current address:
56 Surrey Rd.
London
SE15 3AT, England
Tel and fax: +44 (0)171 639 8146
Email: pgpix@ndirect.co.uk
Web: www.pgpix.ndirect.co.uk

Tomas Utsi Naturfoto AB

Paksuniemi 3064
SE-981 29 Kiruna, Sweden
Tel: +46 (0)980 27000
Fax: +46 (0)980 27077
Mobile: +46 (0)70 2277000
www.naturfoto.com

Tomas Utsi

"THE LOW SUN IS A FAITHFUL PARTNER."

The professional photographer Tomas Utsi lives just a few stone-throws from Icehotel. Since 1990, he has been living in the neighbouring village of Paksuniemi, along the road to the space research centre, ESRANGE. Tomas was born and raised in the Kiruna area and has worked in the sawmill and forest industry. In 1990 he became a professional photographer.

"I've never gone to any kind of school to learn how to take photographs," he says. "Poor marks were the result of my suffering through years of compulsory school. That's probably why I became a photographer!"

In the 1980s an interest in landscape and nature drew his attention to issues of environmental destruction. "The anxiety it caused me became so oppressive and destructive that I needed some kind of relief." Tomas discovered that his safety valve was through the lens of a camera.

"I think that whatever medium you choose, you should have some sort of commitment to a particular subject. Just having photography as your only passion can't be all that interesting or productive."

Tomas Utsi sees Kiruna as a centre of strange occurrences and unusual relationships in nature.

"Anyone who works in the visual arts up here in the north has the low Sun as a faithful partner. The most pleasing light comes when the Sun is near the horizon. Its rays must pass through a very great deal of air, which makes the light soft and diffuse, and it takes on a red hue at a dramatically low angle. Because the Sun's path is so flat north of the Arctic Circle, the low light lasts a long time, both in terms of the day and the year. I'm fortunate to be able to take photographs at this latitude," concludes Tomas Utsi .

Torbjörn Lövgren

"NORTHERN LIGHTS PHOTOGRAPHER"

These are just a few examples of Torbjörn Lövgren's long list of achievements:

- Multi-image slide show during Norrland Week, World Expo Seville, 1992.
- Invitations to Höfn in Iceland and Irkutsk in Russia.
- Show of Northern Lights photos, Moderna Museet, Stockholm, summer 1994.
- Numerous national and international exhibitions, TV programmes, photo features on a range of topics from wildlife to industry.
- Books by himself and others.
- Record labels with aurora borealis for ABBA and Polar Records, some of his most widely distributed work.

Torbjörn Lövgren uses Hasselblad, Nikon, and Canon equipment.

Address: Torbjörn Lövgren
SE-981 00 Kiruna, Sweden
Tel: +46 980-180 13
Mobile: +46 70 33 99 013
Email: torbjorn.lovgren@swipnet.se
http://www.lovgrensfoto.com

He is acknowledged as one of the world's very best Northern Lights photographers. Many of his fantastic pictures of the shimmering aurora borealis have appeared in books, periodicals, exhibitions and multi-image slide shows. It is no exaggeration to state that Torbjörn Lövgren is one of the world's leading specialists in the art and science of Northern Lights photography.

In 1964 he began work at what was then known as the Kiruna Geophysical Observatory (now IRF, the Swedish Institute of Space Physics) in Kiruna. This was the start of a successful career for the self-taught photographer from the tiny village of Junosuando in Tornedalen. However, he was not employed as a photographer, but as a technician.

"Nobody at the Geophysical Observatory could develop slides for the researchers," explains Torbjörn Lövgren. "I became interested in photography during an eight-month stay in hospital, in 1961. What began as a hobby soon developed into a full-time job. Technically, photography was becoming more and more advanced, and I took one course after another.

In 1967 one of the researchers was doing a PhD on the Northern Lights and I was put in charge of the instruments, out in the woods. I was spending five or six hours a night under the clear skies. Once all the gear was working properly, I had nothing else to do, so I started taking pictures of the Northern Lights. They had always fascinated me. That's how it all happened."

Like many other famous photographers working in the Kiruna area who have documented the beauty and culture of Lapland (Borg Mesch, Sven Hörnell and others), Torbjörn has spent literally years outdoors watching the shifting of the Eight Seasons. Through snow and ice in the bitter cold of winter, and in the warm and bright summer nights, he has carried his equipment in search of that perfect picture of the magical light of Lapland. Many of his captivating photographs have fascinated people the world over.

"Taking pictures of the Northern Lights is not particularly difficult if you find yourself in the right place at the right time with the right equipment. The best time is from mid-September until mid-April. Otherwise, it's just too light at night."

He carries a tripod, preferably a manual camera with a B function on the shutter, light-sensitive film (400 ASA) and a lens with about a 2.0 aperture.

"The timing depends on how intense the Lights are, and if there's snow, moonlight and any reflection from the water. A good rule of thumb is about 20 seconds," Torbjörn recommends to anyone who is thinking of photographing the celestial phenomenon.

Fotografen i Kiruna AB

Kenneth Paulsson
Box 259, SE-981 23 Kiruna, Sweden
Tel: +46 980-833 00
Mobile: +46 70 644 4000
Email: fotografen@kiruna.se
http://www.photosweden.com

Kenneth Paulsson

"…THE MOMENT COMES CRAWLING AT A SNAIL'S PACE…"

By the age of 15 Kenneth Paulsson was taking photographs for local newspapers. Since then, he has worked as a professional photographer in a great variety of contexts. He is now widely known as "the Photographer from Kiruna", which is more or less the name of his company, Fotografen i Kiruna. In 1988 he opened his own studio, in which countless portraits of wedding couples, confirmands and little children as well as innumerable advertising photos have been taken over the years.

He can sometimes be quite difficult to reach. When that happens, it is almost certain that something important is happening somewhere in northern Sweden. Kenneth Paulsson is often the first person to arrive at the scene. That explains why his press photos appear frequently in Norrländska Socialdemokraten, one of the regional newspapers, or in the evening papers. Kenneth knows that a photographer must be alert if he or she is to capture an event the very instant it happens. News comes creeping at a snail's pace but vanishes in a flash. Photojournalism is his great passion. After all his years in the field and in the studio he has learnt a thing or two about people, and how to get them to relax and act naturally in front of a camera. "It makes the pictures so much better," he says. When not on an assignment of his own, he may well be out shooting for the New York Times, The European or the Swedish agency Pressens Bild. He once did a spread for Life Magazine.

Kenneth is an all-weather photographer. Rain or shine, he's out there. In January 1999 the temperature dropped to a record low -54°C (-65°F) in Karesuando. Kenneth captured the moment on film. That same year, southern Sweden experienced record-breaking summer temperatures. And there he was, sweating it out behind his camera.

"The trick is not to notice whether your fingers are stiff with cold or the sweat is rolling down your forehead. The camera must be kept in perfect focus and nothing can be allowed to go wrong."

Mark Wilcox, Translator

Mark Wilcox, a freelance writer and translator, came to Sweden from Canada in 1984. After thirteen years in Norrbotten, Lapland, he and his family made the difficult decision to trade their northern lifestyle for a much different way of life in the south of Sweden. Mark began his career as an English language teacher and training consultant, but became successively more involved, as a copywriter, in marketing and public relations. Over the years he has helped countless individuals, companies and organisations to communicate effectively in the international arena, and has contributed to numerous export successes. Mark is currently living in Höganäs, Sweden. *email: mwilcox@telia.com*

A WORD OF THANKS

Essentially, most people subscribe to one of three attitudes here in life. Some people initiate and realise successful projects; some take part in projects that others have started, while a third category includes those who shake their heads and doubt that anything can be possible, least of all wild ideas.

All those involved in making this book about Icehotel a reality know that dreams can be made to come true. I would like to offer a big thank you to all those who have dared to take that step from thought to action.

Pär Granlund

Kraftverket is an ideas and communications agency, where six studios (architecture, design, innovation, communication, lighting & new media) develop clients individually and jointly. The company's business concept is to gather people with the right skills in the area of communications within a single forum to carry out successful, all-encompassing communication projects.

Under a single brand, about thirty creators and innovators are currently working on product development, packaging, project planning, flash programming, marketing, strategy, interior decoration, concept development, design and integration. Kraftverket's current clients include Hewlett-Packard, Ericsson, Manpower, NCC, Cap Gemini, Martela, Kemetyl, Stockholm Transport, Connect Things and Severa Pet Foods.

And a special thanks to my friends Kerstin Andersson, Karin Åberg, Birgitta Möller and Per Ekström, without whose support this book would have remained merely another good intention. Thanks also to Anders Hammarström, awj Kunskapsföretaget AB.